A JOURNAL
FOR FARTS OF
ALL SIZES.

IF LOST, RETURN TO:

_____

_____

_____

AND FAMILY HEIRLOOM

VOLUME ☐ OF ☐

STARTED ON:

COMPLETED ON:

NOTABLE FART · NUMBER 1

DATE

LOCATION

A SUMMARY OF THE EXPERIENCE

☆ ☆ ☆ ☆ ☆ RATING

NOTABLE FART · NUMBER 2

DATE

LOCATION

A SUMMARY OF THE EXPERIENCE

RATING ☆☆☆☆☆

DATE

LOCATION

A SUMMARY OF THE EXPERIENCE

☆☆☆☆☆ RATING

DATE

LOCATION

A SUMMARY OF THE EXPERIENCE

RATING ☆☆☆☆☆

DATE

LOCATION

A SUMMARY OF THE EXPERIENCE

☆☆☆☆☆ RATING

NOTABLE FART · NUMBER 6

DATE

LOCATION

A SUMMARY OF THE EXPERIENCE

RATING ☆☆☆☆☆

DATE

LOCATION

A SUMMARY OF THE EXPERIENCE

☆☆☆☆☆ RATING

NOTABLE FART · NUMBER 8

DATE

LOCATION

A SUMMARY OF THE EXPERIENCE

RATING ☆☆☆☆☆

NOTABLE FART · NUMBER 9

DATE

LOCATION

A SUMMARY OF THE EXPERIENCE

☆☆☆☆☆ **RATING**

DATE

LOCATION

A SUMMARY OF THE EXPERIENCE

RATING ☆☆☆☆☆

NOTABLE FART · NUMBER 11

DATE

LOCATION

A SUMMARY OF THE EXPERIENCE

☆☆☆☆☆ RATING

NOTABLE FART · NUMBER 16

DATE

LOCATION

A SUMMARY OF THE EXPERIENCE

RATING ☆☆☆☆☆

NOTABLE FART · NUMBER 17

DATE

LOCATION

A SUMMARY OF THE EXPERIENCE

☆☆☆☆☆ RATING

DATE

LOCATION

A SUMMARY OF THE EXPERIENCE

RATING ☆☆☆☆☆

NOTABLE FART • NUMBER 19

DATE

LOCATION

A SUMMARY OF THE EXPERIENCE

☆☆☆☆☆ RATING

DATE

LOCATION

A SUMMARY OF THE EXPERIENCE

RATING ☆☆☆☆☆

NOTABLE FART · NUMBER 21

DATE

LOCATION

A SUMMARY OF THE EXPERIENCE

☆☆☆☆☆ RATING

NOTABLE FART · NUMBER 22

DATE

LOCATION

A SUMMARY OF THE EXPERIENCE

RATING ☆☆☆☆☆

NOTABLE FART · NUMBER 23

DATE

LOCATION

A SUMMARY OF THE EXPERIENCE

☆☆☆☆☆ RATING

NOTABLE FART · NUMBER 24

DATE

LOCATION

A SUMMARY OF THE EXPERIENCE

RATING ☆☆☆☆☆

NOTABLE FART · NUMBER 25

DATE

LOCATION

A SUMMARY OF THE EXPERIENCE

☆☆☆☆☆ RATING

DATE

LOCATION

A SUMMARY OF THE EXPERIENCE

RATING ☆☆☆☆☆

NOTABLE FART · NUMBER 27

DATE

LOCATION

A SUMMARY OF THE EXPERIENCE

☆☆☆☆☆ **RATING**

NOTABLE FART · NUMBER 28

DATE

LOCATION

A SUMMARY OF THE EXPERIENCE

RATING ☆☆☆☆☆

NOTABLE FART · NUMBER 29

DATE

LOCATION

A SUMMARY OF THE EXPERIENCE

☆☆☆☆☆ RATING

DATE

LOCATION

A SUMMARY OF THE EXPERIENCE

RATING ☆☆☆☆☆

DATE

LOCATION

A SUMMARY OF THE EXPERIENCE

☆ ☆ ☆ ☆ ☆ RATING

NOTABLE FART · NUMBER 32

DATE

LOCATION

A SUMMARY OF THE EXPERIENCE

RATING ☆☆☆☆☆

DATE

LOCATION

A SUMMARY OF THE EXPERIENCE

☆☆☆☆☆ RATING

NOTABLE FART · NUMBER 34

DATE

LOCATION

A SUMMARY OF THE EXPERIENCE

RATING ☆☆☆☆☆

DATE

LOCATION

A SUMMARY OF THE EXPERIENCE

☆☆☆☆☆ RATING

NOTABLE FART · NUMBER 36

DATE

LOCATION

A SUMMARY OF THE EXPERIENCE

RATING ☆☆☆☆☆

DATE

LOCATION

A SUMMARY OF THE EXPERIENCE

☆☆☆☆☆ RATING

DATE

LOCATION

A SUMMARY OF THE EXPERIENCE

RATING ☆☆☆☆☆

NOTABLE FART · NUMBER 45

DATE

LOCATION

A SUMMARY OF THE EXPERIENCE

☆☆☆☆☆ RATING

NOTABLE FART · NUMBER 46

DATE

LOCATION

A SUMMARY OF THE EXPERIENCE

RATING ☆☆☆☆☆

DATE

LOCATION

A SUMMARY OF THE EXPERIENCE

☆ ☆ ☆ ☆ ☆ RATING

DATE

LOCATION

A SUMMARY OF THE EXPERIENCE

RATING ☆☆☆☆☆

NOTABLE FART · NUMBER 49

DATE

LOCATION

A SUMMARY OF THE EXPERIENCE

☆☆☆☆☆ RATING

DATE

LOCATION

A SUMMARY OF THE EXPERIENCE

RATING ☆☆☆☆☆

DATE

LOCATION

A SUMMARY OF THE EXPERIENCE

☆☆☆☆☆ RATING

DATE

LOCATION

A SUMMARY OF THE EXPERIENCE

RATING ☆☆☆☆☆

DATE

LOCATION

A SUMMARY OF THE EXPERIENCE

☆☆☆☆☆ RATING

NOTABLE FART · NUMBER 54

DATE

LOCATION

A SUMMARY OF THE EXPERIENCE

RATING ☆☆☆☆☆

NOTABLE FART · NUMBER 55

DATE

LOCATION

A SUMMARY OF THE EXPERIENCE

☆☆☆☆☆ RATING

DATE

LOCATION

A SUMMARY OF THE EXPERIENCE

RATING ☆☆☆☆☆

DATE

LOCATION

A SUMMARY OF THE EXPERIENCE

☆☆☆☆☆ RATING

DATE

LOCATION

A SUMMARY OF THE EXPERIENCE

RATING ☆☆☆☆☆

NOTABLE FART · NUMBER 59

DATE

LOCATION

A SUMMARY OF THE EXPERIENCE

☆☆☆☆☆ RATING

DATE

LOCATION

A SUMMARY OF THE EXPERIENCE

RATING ☆ ☆ ☆ ☆ ☆

DATE

LOCATION

A SUMMARY OF THE EXPERIENCE

☆☆☆☆☆ RATING

NOTABLE FART · NUMBER 62

DATE

LOCATION

A SUMMARY OF THE EXPERIENCE

RATING ☆☆☆☆☆

DATE

LOCATION

A SUMMARY OF THE EXPERIENCE

☆☆☆☆☆ RATING

NOTABLE FART · NUMBER 39

DATE

LOCATION

A SUMMARY OF THE EXPERIENCE

☆☆☆☆☆ RATING

NOTABLE FART · NUMBER 38

DATE

LOCATION

A SUMMARY OF THE EXPERIENCE

RATING ☆☆☆☆☆

NOTABLE FART · NUMBER 43

DATE

LOCATION

A SUMMARY OF THE EXPERIENCE

☆☆☆☆☆ RATING

NOTABLE FART · NUMBER 42

DATE

LOCATION

A SUMMARY OF THE EXPERIENCE

RATING ☆☆☆☆☆

NOTABLE FART · NUMBER 41

DATE

LOCATION

A SUMMARY OF THE EXPERIENCE

☆☆☆☆☆ RATING

NOTABLE FART · NUMBER 40

DATE

LOCATION

A SUMMARY OF THE EXPERIENCE

RATING ☆☆☆☆☆

NOTABLE FART · NUMBER 64

DATE

LOCATION

A SUMMARY OF THE EXPERIENCE

RATING ☆☆☆☆☆

NOTABLE FART · NUMBER 65

DATE

LOCATION

A SUMMARY OF THE EXPERIENCE

☆☆☆☆☆ RATING

NOTABLE FART · NUMBER 66

DATE

LOCATION

A SUMMARY OF THE EXPERIENCE

RATING ☆☆☆☆☆

DATE

LOCATION

A SUMMARY OF THE EXPERIENCE

☆☆☆☆☆ RATING

NOTABLE FART · NUMBER 68

DATE

LOCATION

A SUMMARY OF THE EXPERIENCE

RATING ☆☆☆☆☆

DATE

LOCATION

A SUMMARY OF THE EXPERIENCE

☆ ☆ ☆ ☆ ☆ RATING

NOTABLE FART · NUMBER 70

DATE

LOCATION

A SUMMARY OF THE EXPERIENCE

RATING ☆☆☆☆☆

DATE

LOCATION

A SUMMARY OF THE EXPERIENCE

☆☆☆☆☆ RATING

NOTABLE FART · NUMBER 72

DATE

LOCATION

A SUMMARY OF THE EXPERIENCE

RATING ☆☆☆☆☆

DATE

LOCATION

A SUMMARY OF THE EXPERIENCE

☆☆☆☆☆ RATING

NOTABLE FART · NUMBER 74

DATE

LOCATION

A SUMMARY OF THE EXPERIENCE

RATING ☆☆☆☆☆

DATE

LOCATION

A SUMMARY OF THE EXPERIENCE

☆☆☆☆☆ **RATING**

NOTABLE FART · NUMBER 76

DATE

LOCATION

A SUMMARY OF THE EXPERIENCE

RATING ☆☆☆☆☆

NOTABLE FART · NUMBER 77

DATE

LOCATION

A SUMMARY OF THE EXPERIENCE

☆☆☆☆☆ RATING

DATE

LOCATION

A SUMMARY OF THE EXPERIENCE

RATING ☆☆☆☆☆

DATE

LOCATION

A SUMMARY OF THE EXPERIENCE

☆☆☆☆☆ RATING

NOTABLE FART · NUMBER 80

DATE

LOCATION

A SUMMARY OF THE EXPERIENCE

RATING ☆☆☆☆☆

NOTABLE FART · NUMBER 81

DATE

LOCATION

A SUMMARY OF THE EXPERIENCE

☆☆☆☆☆ RATING

DATE

LOCATION

A SUMMARY OF THE EXPERIENCE

RATING ☆☆☆☆☆

NOTABLE FART · NUMBER 83

DATE

LOCATION

A SUMMARY OF THE EXPERIENCE

☆☆☆☆☆ RATING

NOTABLE FART · NUMBER 84

DATE

LOCATION

A SUMMARY OF THE EXPERIENCE

RATING ☆☆☆☆☆

DATE

LOCATION

A SUMMARY OF THE EXPERIENCE

☆☆☆☆☆ RATING

DATE

LOCATION

A SUMMARY OF THE EXPERIENCE

RATING ☆☆☆☆☆

NOTABLE FART · NUMBER 87

DATE

LOCATION

A SUMMARY OF THE EXPERIENCE

☆☆☆☆☆ RATING

DATE

LOCATION

A SUMMARY OF THE EXPERIENCE

RATING ☆ ☆ ☆ ☆ ☆

DATE

LOCATION

A SUMMARY OF THE EXPERIENCE

☆☆☆☆☆ RATING